D0885507

At Sea

poems by

Rebekah Bloyd

Finishing Line Press
Georgetown, Kentucky

At Sea

ACKNOWLEDGMENTS

Great thanks to the editors and readers of these journals, in which some of the
poems appeared, sometimes in slightly different form:

"Adrift / All is Not Lost," *The Cincinnati Review*
"La Playa Grande," *Five Fingers Review*
"Mother and Son at Home, Mérida, Venezuela," *Narrative Magazine*
"Mi Otro Yo," *Pinyon Review*
"Contract Extended, West Indies," *Spirit Wind Poetry Gallery*
"New World Warblers," and "At Sea," *Spolia*
"Regresa a La Casa de Carlos Hurtado," *Quarterly West*

For joining me in serio ludere on an early draft of the poem "At Sea," special
thanks go to Kelly McMahon, of May Day Studio.

For joining me in lifting words off the page into life, heartfelt thanks go to SBS.

Publisher: Leah Maines
Editor: Christen Kincaid
Cover Art: Anke Burger
Author Photo: Jim Norrena

Printed in the USA on acid-free paper.
Order online: www.finishinglinepress.com
            also available on amazon.com

Author inquiries and mail orders:
Finishing Line Press
P. O. Box 1626
Georgetown, Kentucky 40324
U. S. A.

Contents

Adrift / All is Not Lost

He kept the things that were best. Things blue, and white, and the colors of skin in Caracas, Buenos Aires, Toronto, Cincinnati, San Francisco. He kept them poorly; he threw away the translucent box cover for the book on the body I'd given him, the one so dear I'd returned to the shop's shelves my own selections.

Home to our Belvedere house just off Haight, to my office with the desk painted red, the bookshelves filled with spine after spine arranged by him. I entered the room after we'd moved and saw it like that: the red desk, the filled shelves. He'd done that for me, made the room that beautiful. I could not leave right away.

Tonight I searched the shelves of my San José life for the Great White. I could find only one with a black cover, a Scribner's edition belonging to my husband.

But he was my husband once, my Great Brown man with the silver pedigree. He took the blue-bound sea with him, the cover in tatters, the notes of others before me in the book, my notes in the margins, margins the place he left room.

He took the notes with him, and The Beatles' Great White Album, the one first belonging to my brother Jonn, then belonging to me. He made sure to be gone from the house when I came looking for the last things. I keep my eyes on the sea.

La Playa Grande

i

She sees him crash harder than the surf into the shore, knees and fists carve holes in the sand when his boy's body rolls to rest. The sea pulls away. A few bathers stroll around his contortions. Small moons set, rise crying from the waves, dunked for the first time. Venezuelan beauties in string bikinis arch and flip next to bronzed beer bellies in beach chairs, parked by Polar-full coolers. Under his own incantation, the boy crashes harder than the surf.

At age six, the sea air was brought to me in a metal box that hummed on my chest, pale underneath the hospital gown. A machine that exhaled salty air to coat the cavities pneumonia had opened.

ii

Body low to the sand, the boy scrambles in on bent fours, persistent in his efforts to come from the sea as a crab. Moon cries continue. Near the overlook, a young man builds a turquoise towel nest, invites in his shivering companion. Pulled from silver-quilted depths, in vendors' hands glass jars of marinated squid shine. A boy extends his study of crabness.

I filled my lungs as fully as I could, following the good doctor's advice, thinking it wasn't so bad, this sea air. Not caring for a sea I'd never seen.

iii

His raw boy's body rolls to rest. He elbows his way to dry sand, props his head on his claws.

On the promontory, she closes her eyes, takes one step seaward. Raises her freckled arms from her sides and imagines herself as the capital letter T and what she might go To. She fills her lungs with sea air, increasingly familiar, still promising.

Mother and Son at Home, Mérida, Venezuela

Among his Lego blocks
scattered on a patio,
fingerlings flash and dart,

regroup, then snap minuscule
red and blue scutes onto the back
of an armored Titanosaur, a giant herbivore

who would not swap the constant spring
of Mérida's valley, the sparkling shallows
hung with afternoon shadows

for the snowcapped
Espejo, Bonpland, Bolívar, and Humboldt,

ceramic bowls turned upside
down. He shivers at the thought.

> "Mijo, do you have to finish the creature
> outside?"
>
> "Mamá, it's nearly alive."

Mi Otro Yo

First wet with dirt, now dusty,
now a hot upheaval of tar
spiraling down to Caracas, you take the road
and then its offer: una pastelería
and its shaded counter, a place to pause,
to take un jugo de tamarindo,
un café cortado before continuing.
The office will be open, its lounge half empty
of the humid air that lingers.
An hour will pass before
someone is ready to see you.

You see a cracked and muddled
sadness coat the rubble
behind the building, back of another
rascacielo of red steel lines and bright blue
balconies that climb floor by floor
toward a final space. And higher still
spin giant prizes that tug
away at anger: una arepa dominó,
una botella de Johnny Walker,
una Aspirina Bayer.

An hour passes. A teenaged boy approaches
the lounge window, gestures
it's you someone will see now. Sigue,
mi hermano, he says, imagining
you would not approve of the T-shirt
he owns, the one popular this year
that line after line, until its premature
hem, condemns: *los jefes   las secretarias*
los vendedores   las líneas   la gasolina
las calles   los huecos   el tráfico
los impuestos   los bancos   la corrupción
las condiciones of every day
that make a person
wild to fly.

You have been seen. You picture yourself an hour
from now, as you wait for a bus
to grind its way forward, sighting El Avila's
looming greenness ahead, scanning the wall
where sky signs and street paths
converge. Graffiti scrawls
out the days that are simply days,
no release from earth's traffic,
days one after the other, black and night blue,
fresh claw marks on cement. The odd
                    silver streak
          passes through.
                              Acompáñame.
          Tu eres mi otro yo.
Rosa.

Regresa a La Casa de Carlos Hurtado

after a photograph by Federico Vegas

At his first glance, this place on earth appears
still.
                  A shadow cast by—he advances—
the two o'clock sun neatly outlines
the baked mud house, the cují yaque wood
standing together fence piece
by fence piece. He. His father.

          Two wind-roughed trees
brush with scrubby green the scorched straw
roof, continue alongside, as if the salve
they incline to seals the edges
of the dwelling.

Discreet in its grey
ticked suit, a lizard hovers—now there, now here—
near the sill. The window's opened black
reveals the insolubility of sea,
the window's shuttered marine blue
a solid sea. Puzzling one to the other.

The door's human-sooted patch, just above
the handle, hums of palms
and dust.
                    This place in Paraguaná
comes with one admonition,
the antenna skimming the roof's apex,
a long metal tube skewered
by smaller pieces. Xs, crosses, barbed wire knots.
Accounts of the past among which
                              —he grasps—
       an approach must be chosen.

Contract Extended, West Indies

One of those who stays for awhile, he
leaves the after-lunch retaining wall
       fiasco for daybreak's split.

      Returns to the Courtleigh Hotel's
own staging area, the veranda bar
mercifully near his by-the-month room, plans

alternately splayed then curled
loosely like his grasp on brown glass.
      Jamaica's an old quilted cooler.

      The Red Stripe bottle, too, repeats
until a wet crescent shines beyond the ken
of the newly-arrived: "Don't you hit the beach?"

      "I'll quit after the next one."

New World Warblers

In the company of yellow birds, parrotfish,
a handful of friendly locals and outsiders
for three high seasons and the stormy nor'westers

in between, our bodies met. Blessed
with the flesh and oomph of twenty-somethings,
quips gave way to jokes, jokes to anecdotes during
                              our evening shifts

at the unhurried pace of the two-star resort
only your charismatic manager mother
was frantic to make shine. Beneath a million-

starred sky, you coaxed a tiny moon
onto a metal plate secured to the telescope
you'd set up by the sea wall.
                    Here,
                              you offered.

        Here, Budgie. A genuine New Mexico moon.

Budgie, you'd nicknamed me, warming to a toddler's mistake
of my name. *New Mexico,* where you'd
learned the patterns of the night sky.

Before my island visa ran dry (while yours
would not) we took a room in Miami, dank,
air conditioner shuddering.

Your black hair slipped sleek across my blond-
skinned belly. You rose into my face before rocking
back, eyes closed, whispering as you had before,

Where?

We met anew.

Against oceans and hours we coursed,
spiraled, tucked. And woke, our transit
at the edge of that moon begun.

In the departure lounge,
at my apartment door, near my students' classroom,
through the flat afternoons of my Middle West,

I listened for your clear call.

After fifteen years you appeared
to my retired mother absorbing *USA Today,*

your warm self, convicted
of fraud and conspiracy, floating
an Internet pharmacy from a suburban bedroom
in the Keys.

You, two years in the Pen. Three years for
the magnetic mastermind. *Just what relationship
did she talk him into* my own mother wondered, aloud.

We Take Each Other into Our Arms

for Tim Unger, 1960-2000

The breeze swings the gauzy curtains to the side and I cross
in bare feet floorboards of a porch, or a shifting shore that
feels like vacation. We unfold ideas about

when I will next visit, by what conveyances and schedules
I will travel. The wash of cool wind recalls early morning
in the San Juan Islands more than the Caribbean

where I ride beside my father in a carriage, sheet music
forgotten. "Dad, I left it at home! I'm supposed to have five
pages!" I consider playing from memory. A man kicks and
threatens

from outside the windswept cliff where Dad transmits.
Blue circles illuminate near me, but I can't quite tune them
in. "Notice something small," says Tim, delighted in a tux
with short tails, all glittery.

At Sea

after a painting by Josef Šima

a field of children roars

                                       into a seascape
                      swimming perpendicular
spindly legs
crackling

against royal blue

               closing in on a whale's back end

spindly legs
olive, fig, nectarine flesh

                    against royal blue

away from
groves, orchards, greenwood
      their own dreams

this neon
conflagration
         limbs of spring now ships at sea

do we lament?

a funny home
      daddy prone to ditties

            a dripping child
      darting
            towel on chair

sweet bruised knees
underbelly brimming
           near the tub

                            slate skycloud
                at sea

do we fold up
for our lost first bodies?

Rebekah Bloyd's poetry, essays, creative nonfiction, and translations with the Czech poet and immunologist Miroslav Holub have appeared in *Harper's, The London Times Literary Supplement, Field, Poetry, The Cincinnati Review, Sou'Wester, Catamaran*, and elsewhere. Her poetry collections are *Seabook* (Medúza), *Handsome* (Deconstructed Artichoke Press), and *Sister Island* (Blackberry Press). A recipient of a Hedgebrook Residency as well as Fulbright grants to Jamaica and to the Czech Republic, she has also been invited back to Czech universities to lead seminars on the trickster figure in world myth, on the poetry of Joy Harjo, and on creative nonfiction. With husband Steven Boyd Saum, son Kaleb, and feline friend Callie V., Rebekah makes her home in San José and makes her commute to San Francisco, where she teaches at California College of the Arts.

CPSIA information can be obtained
at www.ICGtesting.com
Printed in the USA
LVHW022021080219
606966LV00001B/50